BAKEMONOGATARI

volume 9

A Vertical Comics Edition

Editing: Ajani Oloye
Translation: Ko Ransom
Production: Grace Lu
Hiroko Mizuno

First published in Japan in 2020 by Kodansha, Ltd., Tokyo
Publication for this English edition arranged through Kodansha, Ltd., Tokyo
English language version produced by Vertical Comics,
an imprint of Kodansha USA Publishing, LLC

Translation provided by Vertical Comics, 2021
Published by Kodansha USA Publishing, LLC, New York

Originally published in Japanese as *BAKEMONOGATARI 9* by Kodansha, Ltd.
BAKEMONOGATARI first serialized in *Weekly Shonen Magazine*,
Kodansha, Ltd., 2017-

ISBN: 978-1-949980-99-8

Manufactured in the United States of America

First Edition

odansha USA Publishing, LLC
1 Park Avenue South
Floor
York, NY 10016
.kodansha.us

al books are distributed through Penguin-Random House Publisher Services.

...the curtain will rise on his battle with Dramaturgy—whether Koyomi likes it or not.
Koyomi Vamp's battle begins.
COMING AUGUST 2021!

Next Volume Preview
BAKEMONOGATARI 10
As Koyomi prepares to fight,
Tsubasa suddenly appears before him.
Though Koyomi can't stop questioning how he should treat her...
CRASHER

Senior year of high school / Currently in the manga

4/29

Tsubasa is bewitched by a cat.

5/8

Koyomi catches Hitagi and learns the secret of her weight.

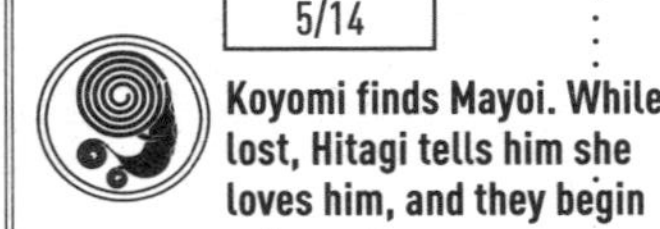

5/14

Koyomi finds Mayoi. While lost, Hitagi tells him she loves him, and they begin going out.

5/29

Koyomi is attacked by Suruga.

6/11

Koyomi and Suruga happen to pass by Nadeko.

6/12

Koyomi and Suruga release Nadeko from the snakes coiled around her.

PRESENT DAY

6/13

Koyomi recollects. . . .

BAKEMONOGATARI: Monster Tale (1) & (2)

1: 240 pages $13.95
2: 330 pages $14.95

Chapter 1: Hitagi Crab / Chapter 2: Mayoi Snail / Chapter 3: Suruga Monkey / Chapter 4: Nadeko Snake

Hitagi Senjogahara, a girl who falls out of the sky toward Koyomi Araragi, weighs so little that she nearly doesn't at all?! Youth is the messiest of times!

BAKEMONOGATARI: Monster Tale (3)

BAKEMONOGATARI
MONSTER TALE PART 03
NISIOISIN
TRANSLATED BY KO RANSOM

226 pages $13.95

Chapter 5: Tsubasa Cat

What is the aberration Koyomi Araragi now faces that has bewitched Tsubasa Hanekawa, the flawless class president?! It's time to mess up your youth!

BAKEMONOGATARI in Detail

The Path of the Manga Until Now

10+ years ago — Mayoi is involved in a traffic accident.

7 years ago — Hitagi falls seriously ill.
She survives, but her mother is sucked into an evil cult.

4 years ago — **Hitagi tries to recruit Suruga to the track team, but Suruga beats her in a free-throw contest.**

2 years ago — Hitagi encounters a crab and has her weight taken from her.

Second year of high school — 3/25 (spring break)

Koyomi meets Tsubasa and etches her panties into his memory. Koyomi encounters a near-death Kiss-Shot and is turned into a vampire.

It shall be...

...thy privilege to aid me.

KIZUMONOGATARI: Wound Tale

354 pages
$14.95

Chapter 0: Koyomi Vamp

It all begins here! It's the prequel to Bakemonogatari: Monster Tale! It all starts on the night following the last day of school, when Koyomi Araragi meets the beautiful vampire Kiss-Shot Acerola-Orion Heart-Under-Blade...

NEKOMONOGATARI: Cat Tale (Black)

288 pages
$15.95

Chapter Nixed: Tsubasa Family

The truth about Golden Week is told at last. What is the aberration that bewitched Tsubasa Hanekawa, the flawless class president? Yet it seems what she's really fallen into...is love.

Continued in Volume 10

I was only after your fortune.
My feelings don't matter.

?!!
M-My family ...
...isn't that rich, you know ?!
...Crap.
I went and cracked a joke.

It felt like I was abusing a kitten.

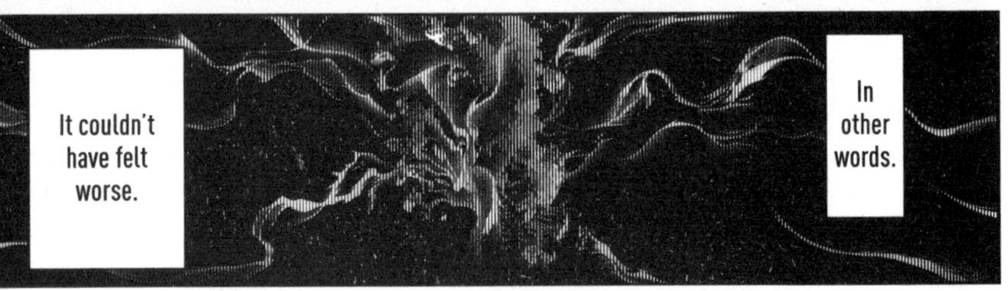
In other words.
It couldn't have felt worse.

...A ...Araragi? Why are you saying these things all of a sudden?
Weren't we having fun talking just a second ago?
It wasn't fun for me at all.
I was pretending.
But—
it was fine.

You're the one who gets on my nerves.

?!

You piss me off.
I'm sick and tired of you.
...

I don't know if this is some way for you to get good letters of recommendation for college, but what do you think you're doing talking to a washout like me?

You might enjoy whatever feelings of superiority you get from this,

but the sight of you standing there feeling sorry for me is unbearable.

Aberrations are like a kind of magnet, you see.

I guess you can say...they *attract*.
Not just anyone... But if you meet the right conditions,
then you get *mixed up* in their magnetic field.

Become **The Aberration Slayer's** thrall, and you'll be pretty powerful in that way as well.
—No.

BULL-
SHIT
...!!

きょとん
HUNH...?
AH

...Um... Sorry. ...Did I say something that touched a nerve?
Ah...
No.
Listen up, Araragi.

Of course, they seemed to be fine out in the sun, plus they had shadows.
I doubt they were vampires, but...
TH-THMP
Situation d'urgence
Wachsamkeit
pericolo
avvertimento
Caution
Danger
Gefahr
危険
警惕
Attenzione
Hm... How do I put it...?
They seemed—very close to it.
TH-THMP
It made me feel like there might just be a real one closer to me than I think.

At first... I thought it was just a rumor.
...Yeah. That's right.
He's right in front of you.
But I may have met a vampire already.
At the station.
...?!

I was stopped by people who seemed like they might be vampires.
They were foreign, and one was a blond hottie.
It was weird. He carried around this gigantic cross.
The other looked like a priest or something, but he seemed kind of suspicious.

And wait—
What are you doing out here at this hour?
Do you live around here?
No, nowhere near. I was taking a stroll
and wondering if I might be able to meet a vampire.

A part of me is really hoping I will.

It was because of this moment ...
...that I decided to continue being human.

...must not realize it now—nor will she ever—
but she saved my life.
That's right.
Hanekawa saved me.

Okay, I got it.
As the person who came up with the idea, I'll take responsibility for checking the videos of the girls' locker room.
I wasn't just talking about the girls' locker room, you know.
DRAT !!
TEE-HEE
Fine, then... I'll let you check the videos of the boys' locker room, so just pretend that I never said that!
NO, THANK YOU!
Hane-kawa ...

"Okay, what might we do to get rid of bullying?"

...

...Like I'd know!! This is supposed to be small talk! Spare me the heavy stuff! She'd toss me that without any sort of advance prep?!

"I know that's pretty heavy, but Araragi, we've got to start somewhere. Like they say, Lourdes wasn't built in a day."

"You mean Rome wasn't—"

Wait.

Didn't "Lourdes" also mean "heavy" in French? A clever one, wasn't she. She ad-libbed that?

"...Um, for starters, placing security cameras throughout a school should get rid of outright bullying at least?"

It wouldn't address the cause, but it'd surely wipe out the effect.

"Hmm. It's not bad as an idea, but there's still the issue of privacy. What about locker rooms?"

"Guh."

She'd pointed out a major flaw in my plan. People do get bullied in locker rooms. In fact, private spaces pose the highest risk.

Despite being a washout, math was the only subject I was good at, but that didn't mean I was at a level where I could discuss it with Hanekawa.

"Unfortunately, all I did today was study Spanish."

"Spanish? ...Hunh. Too bad. I don't know much Spanish."

"Oh. That really is too bad."

"Yeah. Just enough for basic conversations."

...So she could handle basic conversations...

"Anyway, who cares what I studied. Every day is a new lesson for all of us. Let's think more...about...um...yeah—How to make society a better place."

"You're absolutely right about that, Araragi."

Hmm... Well...
Right— here goes.
Araragi, what did you study today?
...
What kind of small talk is that?

I haven't studied any-thing, duh.
No regular high school boy...
...studies during spring break!
I focused mostly on math.
Huh...
If the rumors are true,
she knows her times tables up to five hundred.
Five. Hun-dred.

Not even once have I touched printed matter of such ill repute!
THOK
THOK
HMM.
OH?
I SEE.
THOK
THOK
GRASP
GRASP
I dare not sully my soul with such things.
GRASP
JIGGLE
It was a bald-faced lie.
But Hanekawa let it go at that and spared me a retort.

She's cool like that.
Hey.
Wait!
You walk so fast.
It's not every day that we run into each other—we should take the chance to talk some more.
Talk...?
...I need to hurry.
Reading that aikido book took longer than I thought.
About what?

...
Could she have been running at full speed over a long distance after spotting me...?
...Maybe I'm over-thinking it...
Well—
Yep, that's about it.
SST
THE SKY OF
THE SKY OF AIKIDO
Hm? What's that book?
What's with those eagle eyes?!
Hmm? What's the matter?
Is that book something you don't want me seeing?
Oh!
Could it be something dirty?
Don't be stupid.

That's pretty perverted in its own way.
Hane-kawa...
...was a little out of breath.
Hanekawa, nicknamed "Naoetsu High's grand-prize winner of the genetic lottery,"
was fairly athletic as well. No small task would be able to tire her out.

Pant-
ies?
Oh.
You mean those articles of clothing that are used in this country to protect one's lower body against the cold?
Don't act like you're from a dif- ferent culture.

N- No!
This is a misunder- standing! It's all a misunder- standing!
I only saw the lining of your skirt!
That was the only thing I was paying atten- tion to—the lining of your skirt!

I tried to play it off coolly, but instead, I sounded like I was trying to rap.
Huh?
Did you forget about my panties?
BLOOP
Unfortunately I don't know what you're talking about.
My voice was cracking.

I clearly acted like a guy who knew her panties like the back of my hand.
Even after you stared at them like that...

SKRRK
Wh —
SKKRK
Wh-
Wh-
Wh
—
SKKRK
Wh-
Wh-
Wh
Wh
Wh-
Wh-
Wh!
SKKRK
Wh-Wh-
Wh-What
do you...
...m-m-mean
m-mean m-mean
mean b-b-b-by
th-th-that?

LUNKHEAD
DRAMATURGY
DUMMY
EPISODE
GLOOMY
GUILLOTINE CUTTER
BAKEMONO-
GATARI (9)

LUNKHEAD
DRAMATURGY
DUMMY
EPISODE
BAKEMONO-
GATARI (9)
GLOOMY
GUILLOTINE CUTTER

Oh.
OH, NO.
I'M NOT GIVING YOU A LOOK TODAY.
NGFFT
TH-THWUMP

THWAP
Why are you out here walking the town at this hour like you're one of the Magnificent Seven?
...
...
Hane —!
?
...
kawa
...?
...
...

Good eve-ning, Ara-ragi.

ボロ…
TATTER
THE!! ESSENCE
THE SKY OF AIKIDO
...Oh, no... This cost me 2,500 yen, too...
I was... already dead.
It should have all been over for me when Kiss-Shot sucked me dry of my blood.
So why do I have to fight...?
Aren't I just letting other people use me as they see fit, even in death...?
ESSENCE
Dam-mit ...!
I've got zero moti-vation to do this...
タッ
THP
タッ
THP
タッ
THP
Oh!
I thought it was you!

YAWN
If thou wanted an exit, make a smaller one, fool.
It will let the sunlight in...!
KLATTER

LUNKH

THE SKY OF AIKIDO
The Golden Pavilion?
Mount Fuji?

LUNKHEAD
THE SKY OF AIKIDO
DRAMATURGY
Like you'd find any of that in our town!!

SNRR
...?!
What is the matter, servant?
Oh.
So he departed already.

She bla-tantly ...
...lied to me.
GTT
GTT
361.
GTT
362.
GTT
388.
GTT
389 ...!
March 31.
THE!!
THE SKY OF AIKIDO
A guide with photos for everything from the basics to hidden techniques!
Martial Arts from Around the World That You Can Learn Over-night!
BECOME THE STRONGEST IN HISTORY
THE!!
THE SKY OF AIKIDO

—WAIT, NO, HOLD ON!
DID YOU JUST TRY TO CASUALLY SLIP IN SOMETHING REALLY IMPORTANT JUST NOW?!
The knowledge should be enough on its own, no?
...She barely cares about this.
Oh—that's right.
There was something more important I needed to ask.
...
Hey, Kiss-Shot...
Hm?
Why did you come to Japan...and to a middle-of-nowhere town like here of all places?
For a spot of sightseeing.
It was my wish to see Mount Fuji, the Golden Pavilion, and the like—
That's what she said.

...
Even among plants, huh.
Yeah... it's true.
I always...
...wanted to become a plant—or so I thought, but...

Would that mean—nothing would change even if I became a plant...?
SLUMP
In any case, do be careful not to let him suck thy blood.
Vampires who have their blood sucked by another vampire will see their very existence wrung dry.
...Yeah, I'll be careful...

Or dost thou mean to say that humans do not slay one another?

Uhhh ...

As far as I know, no species of animal exists that does not slay its own kind.
Nay, even among plants.
Trees in a forest fight one another for sunlight and nutrients.

But why would a vampire be a vampire *hunter*?
That doesn't make sense.
KNOCK KNOCK
LUNKHEAD
DRAMATURGY
GUILLOTINE CUTTER
Vampires who slay their own kind are not particularly uncommon.

An eye for an eye.
A tooth for a tooth.
THP
GSSHT
LUNKHEAD
DRAMATURGY
GUILLOTINE CUTTER
BA-GRAKK
A vampire for a vampire.

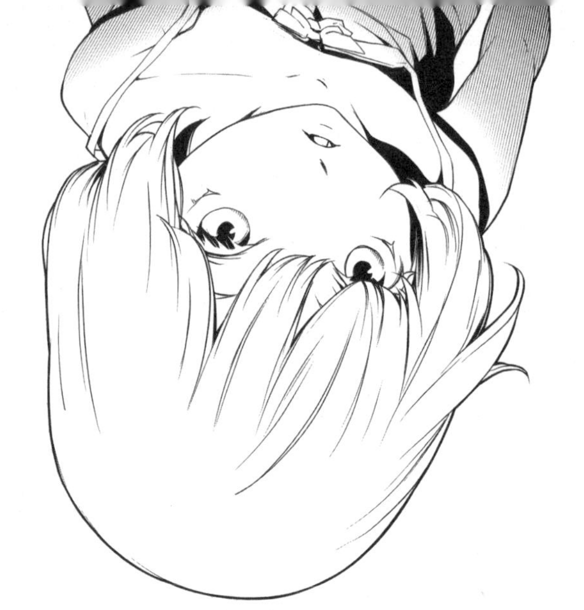

Drama-turgy is a vampire.

...
Huh?
A... vampire?

Couldst thou tell not by the sight of him? Or are there humans who boast his frame?
Never have I heard tell of any in my five hundred years.
Well... No.

Still ...
Wouldn't that make him a traitor?
We've no such concept.

BWOOSH
I think Oshino—
must have already realized something at that point.
BWOOF
After all...
...the story...
...wasn't as simple as I thought.
ZSSHH

It'd be a while later until I learned this,
CRASHER

but Oshino lit his cigarettes— or what looked like them...

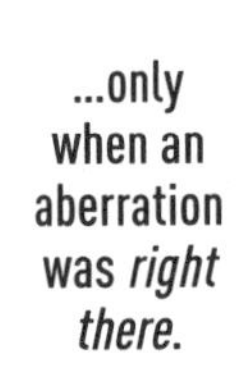
...only when an aberration was *right there*.

He never told me the details,
but that smoke...
...probably protected him, a regular human, from the *bad things*.
FWOOO

BWOOF
They also served *to reveal things that were beyond normal sight*.
I think that's what they're capable of.

Honestly, though... I showed you this abandoned cram school,
I even constructed a barrier to hide you from those guys. I think I've done more than enough...
...But maybe we're also tied together by some kind of fate.
...Oshino. I'm grateful, but...
C'mon. What're you doing there?

Oh... This?
Don't worry. It just looks like this because it's more convenient that way.
This isn't a cigarette.
It's *homa.*

...Homa?
Like incense or some-thing...?
So it relates to that mon-strous SUV?

Apparently, *homa* is something that's used in esoteric Buddhism as a tool for making offerings.

If we're lucky and they do listen, *the game* will be on.
Though it will involve taking on quite a bit of risk on your part.
Huh?
I have been resolved to do so from the start.
That goes for me, of course—and my servant.
She decided… that I was also resolved to do so without my input...
The details are a trade secret, but...I'll ready the playing field.
It would be a little unfair—if Araragi, a *freshly-minted* vampire, had to take on those three battle-hardened veterans at the same time.
In short, we're gonna split those three up.
They won't be a problem for him if he faces them one at a time—that's your read on things, right?
Li'l Heart-Under-Blade.

March 30.
Kiss-Shot began speaking.
It was about last night.
Boy.
Oshino... was it?
All right, then. Tell me thine exact plan to retrieve mine arms and my legs.
I cannot imagine those hunters simply agreeing to negotiate.

TAP
POP
HA HAH.

All I can do is bow my head and ask them nicely. ...In good faith, too.

This is where I've ended up after plenty of twists and turns—
...It kind of feels like... my body's gotten a whole lot sturdier lately...
Though, to be honest, only Oshino knows what's up with each twist and turn—I have no idea why I've ended up in this exact situation.
LUNKHEAD
DRAMATURGY
R.I.P BATTY
In any case, I would first be fighting that man with a massive sword and J(acked)-cup man-boobs.
Drama-turgy.

GRRT
GRRT
GRRT
KREEK
KREEK
KREEK

TWITCH
KLUNK

KREAK

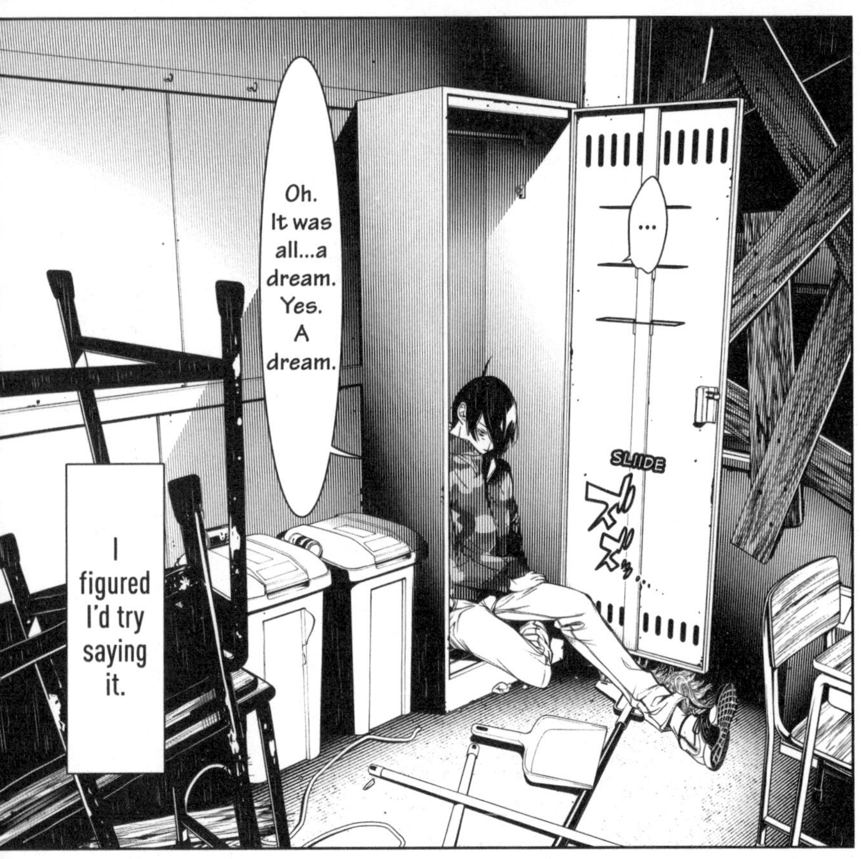
Oh. It was all...a dream. Yes. A dream.
...
SLIIDE
I figured I'd try saying it.

BAKEMONOGATARI

9

BAKEMONOGATARI

9

I'm supposed to be part of the story here...
But it keeps moving forward without me...
MUTTER
I can't trust them... Just can't do it...
MUTTER
Can't trust a single one of them...
MUTTER
SSHT
Good night.
TMP

H-Hold on a second!
You haven't even started to tell us about your exact plan, and now you're talking like some shady salesman...?
And you know... This Oshino guy...
He claims he just happened to be passing by, but...
That has to be a lie!!
Hmph... I cannot ready any human currency for thee, nor do I know the value of such an amount.
I'm sure my servant will prepare the sum even if he must take a loan to do so.
ME ?!
YOU DON'T KNOW WHAT IT'S WORTH, BUT YOU KNOW WHAT A LOAN IS ?!
TAKING ON THAT KIND OF DEBT AT MY AGE IS ENOUGH TO SINK MY ENTIRE FUTURE!
No idea at all... Not even the slight-est...
チャッ
CHKK
チャッ
CHKK
ALWAYS A PLEASURE DOING BUSI-NESS!
AGH! HOLD ON! LOOK AT THAT FACE HE'S MAKING!
AAHH!

Still ...
I gotta say, I like how you do things, Heart-Under-Blade.
You made Araragi your thrall, but you intend to turn him back into a human.
—Right?
...
Oh.
Of course, this would be work for me— I don't do this for free.
Let's see...
How does two million yen or so sound?
TUH
TWO MILLION ?!

I care not for interlopers.
Inter-loper?
I'm the farthest thing from one.
Just said I'm neither friend nor foe, didn't I?
I only stand in between the two sides.
Um... So...
...who exactly is this guy, then...?
Whether you get saved or not is up to you two.

Kiss-Shot's very *existence* — is a little too powerful.
So, her mere presence in a given location causes the balance between this side and the other side to crumble—apparently.
As a self-described specialist in balancing things,
Oshino said that his job was to stand as a neutral party to help negotiate between this side and the other side.
"Exorcisms, hunting—that's not my style.
I'm a pacifist" —Oshino concluded.
Boy.

You see ...
At times, I'm a mysterious vagabond.
At others, I'm a mysterious traveler.
Every now and then, I'm a mysterious wanderer.
On occasion, I'm a mysterious troubadour.
And sometimes, I'm a mysterious nomad of the high sort.
Mysterious through and through, then.
...What are you here for?
...Why do you want to save Kiss-Sh— why do you want to save us?
I get that you're not our enemy.
But you don't seem like much of an ally, either.
Suppose that's only natural when I've got no intention of saving you.
Ha hah —
I'm just trying to balance things out.
Oshino began to explain at last.

SURE, IT'S HARD TO TELL BY THE WAY IT'S DRAWN! YOU COULD SEE THEM AS FLESH-COLORED TIGHTS...
AND WHEN YOU CONSIDER THE SCENES BEFORE AND AFTER THE ONE IN QUESTION, IT DOES MAKE IT LOOK LIKE SHE'S NOT WEARING PANTS!
Sheesh.
They're just drawings, you know.
SHUT UP! THAT'S WHY THEY'RE SO IMPORTANT!! IT'S NOT JUST THE DRAWINGS YOU CAN SEE, IT'S WHAT'S BEHIND THEM, TOO!!
STILL...! YOU CAN'T DO THAT, RIGHT?! I MEAN... NAUSICAA RIDES A MEHVE...
EVERYONE'S GONNA LOOK UP IF YOU'RE ON ONE OF THOSE!
THAT MEANS MITO AND EVEN LORD YUPA WOULD SEE NAU...
AA-AHH!!
YOU KNOW, WE'LL JUST CHALK IT UP TO CULTURE! YEAH, IT'S A DIFFERENCE IN CULTURE!
Ser-vant.
It seems thou hast found a kindred spirit, but who exactly is this fellow?
I do recall him from some-where...
IT'S OSHINO! JUST "OSHINO" IS MORE THAN ENOUGH FOR THIS GUY! NO TITLE NECESSARY! HE DOESN'T DESERVE YOUR RESPECT!!
I can't believe you two. Is that all I am to you?

Hrm? What is the matter?
Thou hast successfully retrieved my body parts, no?
Kiss-Shot...
It sounds like you two know each other... but I just can't trust him.

Oh?

This guy just went straight into the NAUSICAA OF THE VALLEY OF THE WIND NO-PANTS CONTROVERSY with me...!!

Oshino and I wasted time on pointless small talk as we returned.
...And I mean truly pointless... Like about old anime and stuff.
I guess it was to get me to relax and let my guard down...
AH!
THOU HAST RE-TURNED !!
ぴょいん
HOP

If you'd like,
I don't mind interceding.
...
As in?
—This was my first meeting with Mèmè Oshino.
An "expert on aberrations."

...?
...
Wh- What is it?

Noth-ing...
So you call her Kiss-Shot, huh.
Hm?
... Yeah.
Most call her Heart-Under-Blade.
...Huh? Am I calling her by her first name or some-thing...?

Whatever.
She did make you her thrall... I guess it's not too strange.
—In any case, seems like you got yourself into a pretty tricky situation there.

You saved yourself,
Araragi.

...
How... do you know my name...?
Who exactly are you...?

Ha hah. Don't be so guarded. Anyway, let's head back.
...
Head back ...?
To that abandoned cram school. ...I'm the one who told Heart-Under-Blade about it.

Is he ...
Is this guy on my side...?! Or...
You ...
...know Kiss-Shot ...?

ZSSHH
BAM
SWOOSH

Wha...
?!
?
Uh...

Th ...
Thank... you...?
I just happened to be passin' by.
No need to thank me.

You sure are spirited.
Something good happen to you?

GCHHT

Graagh!

GRRK
WHMP
NGH ?!
PTT

TAP
GWOOSH
FWSH
THWNK

BAKE
MONO
GATA
RI 9

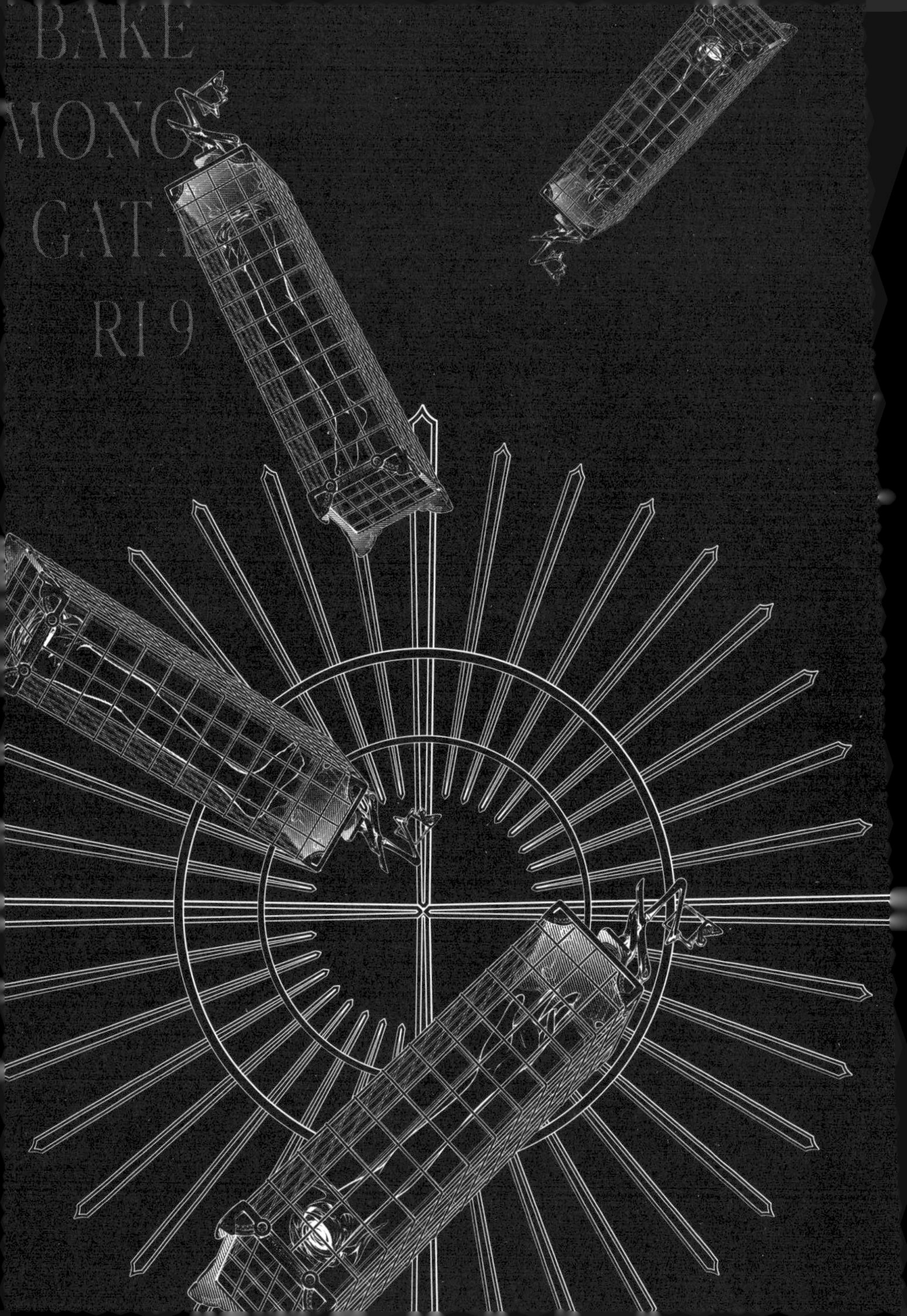
BAKE
MON
GAT
RI 9

FSSSHHH
パキ
KRAK
パキ
KRAK
You sure are spirit-ed.

Something good happen to you?

Is this how she's been treated for the past five hundred years?
Her?
Haah
Haah
Haah
Hooh ...
...
...
?

Leh...
Let's talk—
CHTTR CHTTR
I'd already thrown my life away for Kiss-Shot.
So why ...
...was I clinging onto it so dearly now...?
TREMBLE
TREMBLE
TREMBLE

'Cause I mean, really...

Are you kidding me with this?

Speak the language of the land you're in.
That should go without saying.
Urk!
All right.
The standard approach.
Ah!
Cold.
Smart.
And thorough.
...
Oh... Shit.

Wha...?!
What... is that ...?!
KRRCH
I can't see his face...
...past his man-boobs...
No, no, Mister Dramaturgy.
!!

ZSSHT

—Wait a sec.
Doesn't this mean they saw me as the kind of big brother who was at risk of setting out on a "journey of self-discovery" ...?
PWAP
PAP
PAP
PAP
ZSSHH
AA
AA
AAAAHHHH

They pose no problem for me...?
Guys like that aren't *supposed* to be a problem for me in the first place...
I should've said they're her problem, not mine.

LAA-DE-DA-DE-DAA-DE-DA-DE
AH!
A reply from my little sisters—
New message
From:Little Sisters
Dismiss
Open
They said they would tell people their big brother was making use of his spring break to go on a journey of self-discovery.

Dearest Big Brother,
I know that it's a fact of life to lose our way every now and then. But try to remember...
Where was it that Tyltyl and Mytyl found The Blue Bird of Happiness?
...
Chas-tised by my little sisters...

So...
Doesn't that just mean... they're even stronger than you?
I blundered only because there were three of them.
As much as I hate to admit it... I was utterly unprepared.
I'd presumed I could take even three of their ilk together...
... Huh ...
And I felt a bit absent-minded as well.
I think I was unwell, too.
...
These are just sounding more and more like excuses...
In any case,
faced one at a time, those three pose no problem for thee.
Hah!

But ...
My head's finally starting to cool off, too...
Some-thing's not right. What could it be?
It feels like I'm... over-looking some-thing.
It's not like I believe what Kiss-Shot said—not all of it.
I'll have thee know that I sit among the top rank of vampires.
They call me the aberration slayer.
The aggra-vation slay-er?!
Are you so short-tempered that you kill anything if it so much as annoys you?!
Fool!
Ab-er-ra-tion!!
But those guys took Kiss-Shot's limbs...
...when she was at full power, right...?

Haah!
Haah
Haah
Haah
Haah
Ha-agh...
After running for a while, I decided to stop and catch my breath.
But...
I was certain that I'd run for a few miles, and yet my body was barely—no, actually, it wasn't tired at all.
All the sweat pouring from my body was from a cold sweat—from the rush of escaping.

... Shit.
I thought Heart-Under-Blade had a rule about not making thralls...
Gotta love it.

FSST

Hear the words of God—
and by that I mean, hear these words of mine...
BWOOF
That boy will rue the day...
...he became Heart-Under-Blade's thrall.
...
And if he does and changes his ways...
...are you gonna let him go?
...
The boy is strong—but he is a *fledgling*.
Let us take the *standard approach*. You may act without restraint, Episode.

I only hunt.
Hunting is all I do.
I fix what must be fixed
to correct this world.

And I'm willing to do whatever it takes to achieve that.
GWAAK!
GRAAAGH!
If it takes a blade, a blade is what I shall use. If it takes a monster, then a monster it shall be.
ZHF
FLUTTER
That is all.

You useless fucking bugs! Go back to your shithole of a country !!
WHOOMP! KRUNCH KRUNCH SNAP KRAKKL POP! This is what being stomped to a bloody pulp sounds like. SNAP SNAP SNAP GLURGLE GLURGLE!!!

That's the kind of thing I expected from you.
Based on your charac- ter.
FSSHH
...Why would I need to do something so unpro- ductive?

'Cause you hate them, right?
Monsters like us.
Because you're human.
Hate ?
...No.

KLINK
KLINK

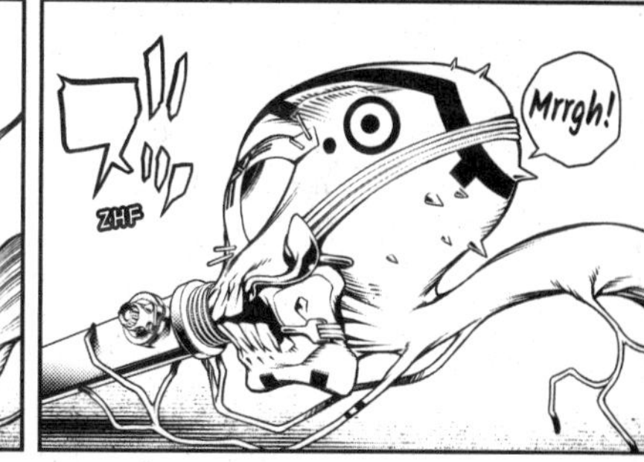
Mrrgh!
ZHF

Nrrrh!
ZLUURCH

I'm disap-pointed in you.

WHMPR
PLRP
WHMPR...
PLRP
PLRP

...
JOLT
SST

BA-KRAK
PYEEE!
No waaay!!
Gimme back...
...my arm!!
SOMEONE STOP HIM!
...
WHIMPER WHIMPER

SNAPPKT
KRASH
Sgree!
SHNK
SHNK
SKRRCH

Stop!
Right!
There!
FFT
Kid!!
KRAK

BWOOOSH
Huh?
!
Agh!

THWAM
THWAM
THWAM
PA-KRAK
Ah!
Hold up.

THWAM
Whoa!

BSSHH
But...
as luck would have it...
AH
A
A
A
A
...they didn't attack me.
...
He doesn't realize you cut off his legs...
...
Tanaka M.D.

GRRK
GRRK
Gyarb!
Blrgh!
GRRK
Unnh!
Unnh!
MUTTER
コク NOD
コク NOD
Grek!
ZWAP

SLURCH

I fell into a com- plete panic.
I don't remember what happened for a good while after.
Hyaa
A
Ee—
A
A
A
But...
given the situation, the course of action I took was the most idiotic one conceivable.
I aban- doned the fight and
showed my back, which was totally unguard- ed—

Let me take care of this, Guillotine Cutter—you greedy bastard.
Haah!
I'll make a clean kill—no permanent damage.
Haah!
Haah!
My organization has a need for him, you see...
...but fine—fair competition will help us improve both our abilities.
Heh. Gotta love it.
Eek!
Eeek!
SCURRY
SCURRY
SCURRY
SCURRY
THP

KREEK

BWOOF
SHHHHNP

...
What do you think you're doing, Episode?
GRK
GRK
GRK
GRRRRCH
FRRSH
I should be asking you the same.
That knife came flying straight for my eyes.
And anyway, we get a separate bounty for slaying him on top of Heart-Under-Blade, right?

It was im-possi-ble.
AAAAAA
AAAA
GH
I was a mere high school student. Even if I did just become a vampire,
you can't just tell me to fight professional vampire hunters. How exactly am I supposed to do that?
And Kiss-Shot was basically telling me I could do it as long as I face them one at a time.
But two are coming out of nowhere to attack me at once! So, that's already become a worthless lie!

Kiss-Shot— told me something.
Faced one at a time,
those three pose no problem for thee.
Hear me!
Thou art now my thrall.
A king of aberrations.

Would I really be able to turn back into a human again?
What proof did I have that Kiss-Shot wasn't lying?
She could just be using me to recover her arms and legs—in fact, wasn't that the most likely scenario?

BAKEMONOGATARI
I think there were a whole host of things...
...that I should have been questioning.
KREE

Who the hell's this guy?!
He's not Heart-Under-Blade!
Hey!
So that monster had a thrall...
This was unexpected, but we should at least be able to get some use out of his body by asking it about her whereabouts.
Let's bring his body back with us in the *smallest pieces possible*.

CRASHER

According to Kiss-Shot...
...she needed to get her limbs back and return to full power to turn me back into a human.
She made it sound so easy—like I'd just stumble into them somehow...
And that the whole thing would probably get settled before tomorrow, but...
Putting aside the question of whether or not I can go back to being a human...
SIGH はぁ...
KRAK
After seeing...
those arms of hers...
CHHK
CHHK
BWOOF

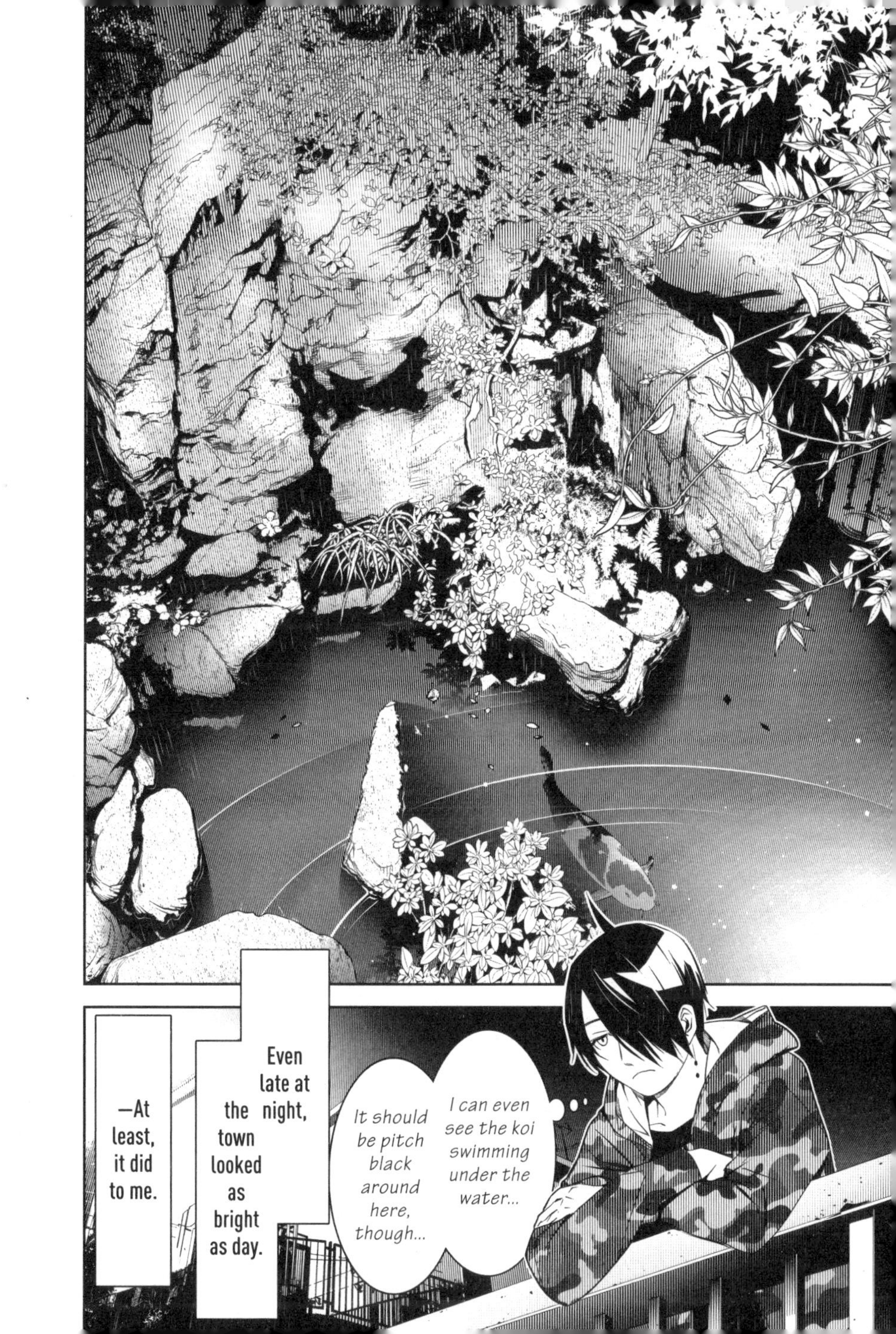
I can even see the koi swimming under the water...
It should be pitch black around here, though...
Even late at night, the town looked as bright as day.
—At least, it did to me.

Meue-nakamachi Station Timetable

Outbound To Urabe		Time	To Oyama
15		5	
17		6	30
11	39	7	07
02	44	8	42
27		9	
19		10	07
		11	
18		12	40
04		13	
		14	

DAMN THIS STUPID, BACKWATER TOWN!

THE NEXT TRAIN DOESN'T COME FOR ANOTHER HOUR!

THAT'S WHY I WAS SAYING WE SHOULD'VE GOTTEN ON THE TRAIN JUST NOW!

Gotta love it.

NO, YOU DON'T! WHY THE HELL'RE YOU STEALING MY CATCH-PHRASE?! DON'T MAKE ME KILL YOU!

A monster, rescuing a human?!
What?!
GRRRRRRRRRKK
GRK
GRK
GRK

YAWN
What a thoughtless thing to say!!
An unforgivable lie! Only humans can rescue humans!
In other words, none other than I, a god, could ever...!
...
SST
FIND
FOUND
FIND
Seems like she's on the move.

abe
To Oyama
Should we really have let her go just like that?
Her and that huge pair of hers?

From the first part of what she said ...
...I can see we think in similar ways.
She's an incredible talent. Straighten her out in the right way, and I might even consider welcoming her as a senior member of my organization.
Hah.

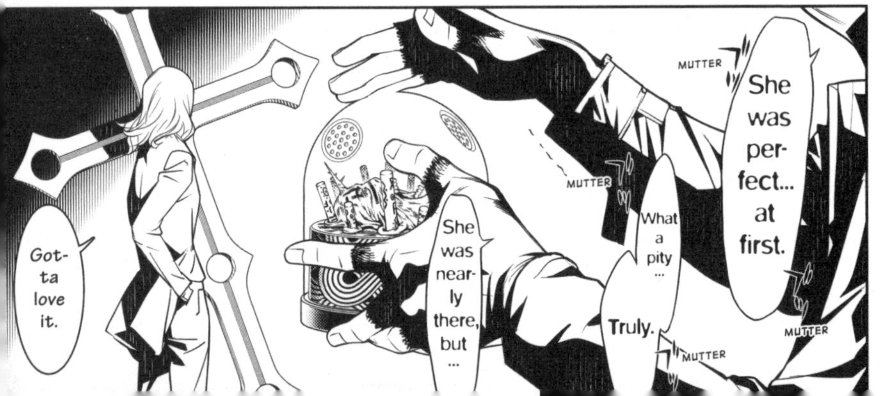
MUTTER
She was per-fect... at first.
MUTTER
What a pity ...
She was near-ly there, but ...
Truly.
MUTTER
MUTTER
Got-ta love it.

ナデ
PAT
ナデ
PAT
ナデ
PAT

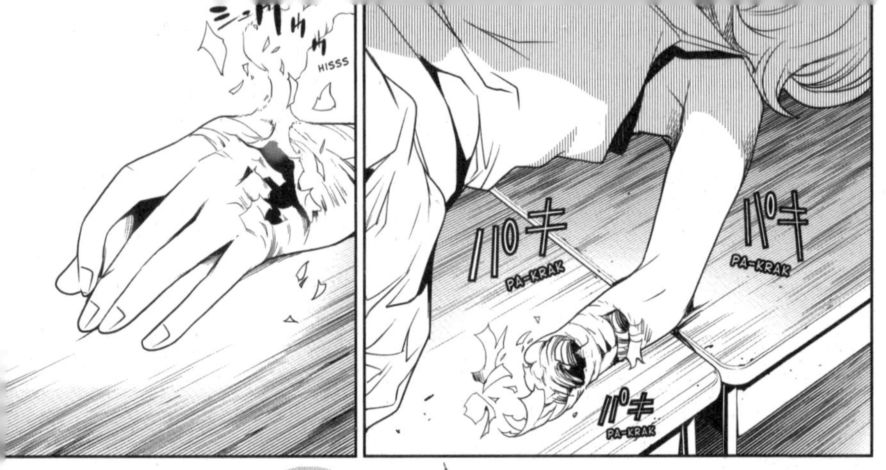
パキ
PA-KRAK
パキ
PA-KRAK
パキ
PA-KRAK
HISSS

I was able to at least form these limbs, but they're empty inside...

SNRRR

—And that's why I'd want...
...to meet that person.

SNRRR

MRGH
SCATTER
TWITCH
SCATTER
SCATTER

I bet they'd save all kinds of people.

They'd save humans and non-humans alike—

anyone who couldn't be saved.

If ... someone like that did exist...
CRUNCH
...they would still be a human being, but one that knows "pain."
CRASHER
And I imagine ...
...they would be kinder than any other.

Very good.
It seems you're a wise woman.
In that case,
let's say someone maintained the intelligence and strength of a human—while acquiring weapons as a part of their body.
HOW WOULD THAT MAKE THEM DIFFERENT FROM A HUMAN?
...
You're not... one of *them*—are you?
You have shadows... And it seems like you're fine being in the sunlight...
Gotta love it.

But by equipping weapons *outside* of their bodies, humans forgot the meaning of pain.
Now that they could kill their opponents without any risk, they could continue slaughtering without end.

That is indeed what makes us humans.
Just as power is what makes a god a god.

The appearance of humans must be nothing short of a calamity for other living creatures.

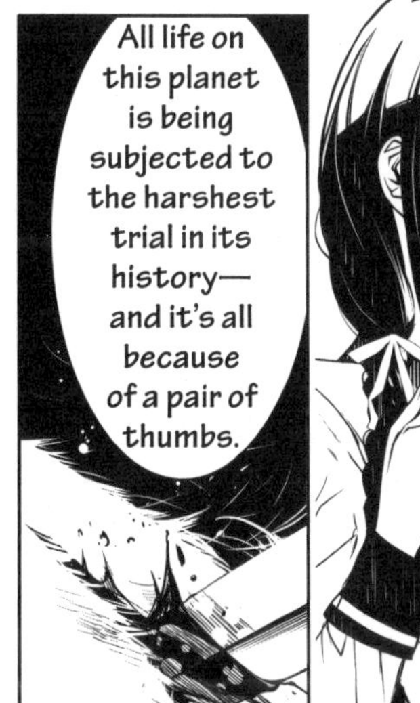
All life on this planet is being subjected to the harshest trial in its history—and it's all because of a pair of thumbs.

Claws.

Fangs.

Or physical abilities—or wings, or scales, or shells, or horns, or... venom.
Living creatures are equipped with their own kinds of powerful weapons.
They evolved to protect themselves from enemies and to feed on other lives.

But using these weapons comes with a risk.
No matter how powerful they may be, they are still a part of the body. Using them excessively brings about pain.
...That is why animals avoid unnec-essary conflict.

Because of this,
mankind lost what we call "pain."

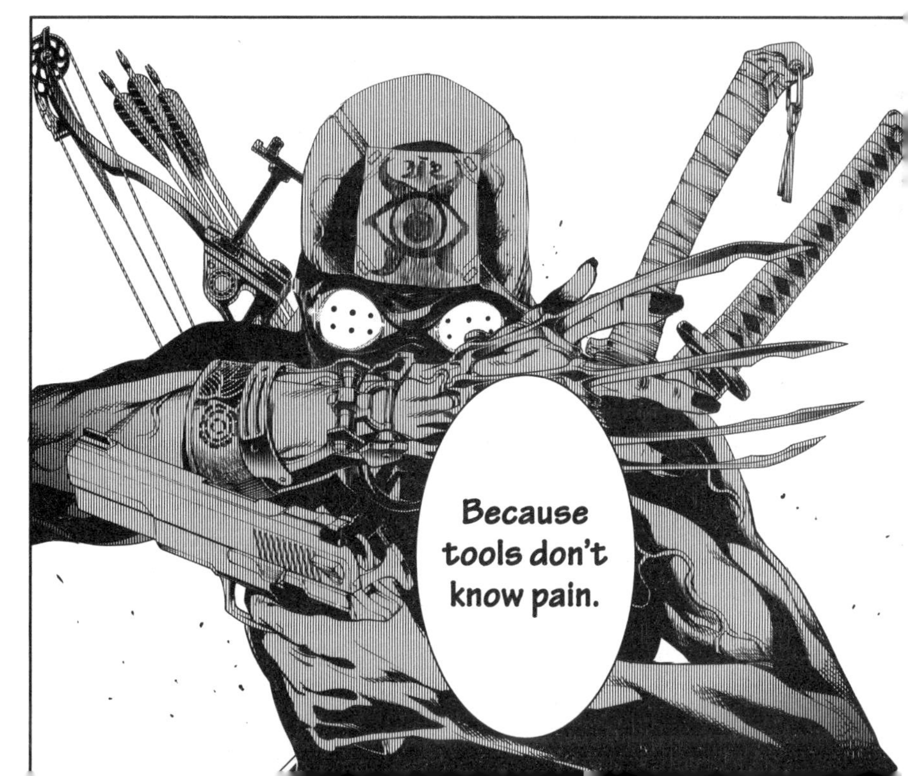
Because tools don't know pain.

No need to worry. Depending on your answer,
you just might find out what it is, whether you want to or not.

...
I...
can only an-swer with what I know.

But the difference between a man and a monkey...
...is a *thumb.*

The human thumb has a muscle that monkeys lack. That muscle, known as the extensor pollicis brevis, allows humans to hold objects.

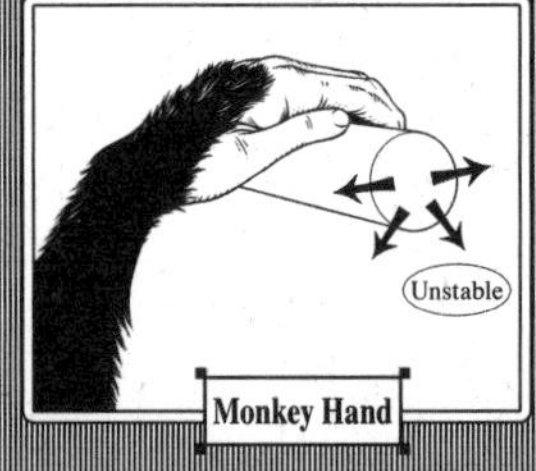

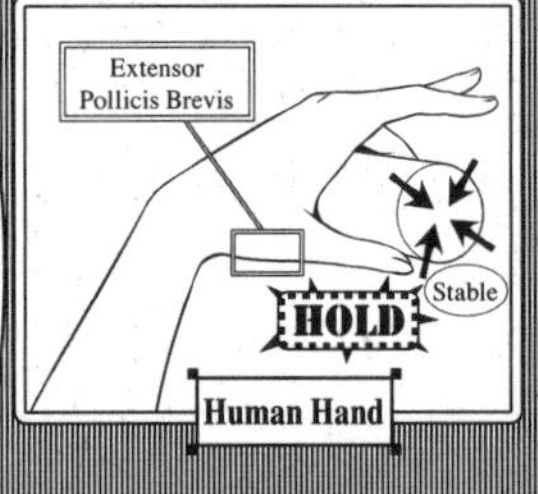

This difference is critical to being able to handle tools.

"It is only right for mon-sters to be exter-minat-ed."
SHHHINK

...
What's that sound?

KREAK
GRIND
GRIND
GRIND
GRIND
GRIND
GRG GRG GRG
JA-KLINK
Kiss-Shot Acerola-Orion Heart-Under-Blade...
...said it so matter-of-factly.

PAT
ナデ
PAT
ナデ
PAT
ナデ

AYE
!
HMPH

AH
!!
Oh no!
I WASN'T THINKING —!

Return to me my limbs.
It will be a simple task for thee as thou art now.
Like asking the king of all beasts to hunt his prey.

...
THP
Thou canst.
Upon my name, I give thee mine assurance.
It is possible for thou to returnest to thy human form.
Aye, possible, but...

To do so, thou must do a bit of work for me.
MASTER
GRATITUDE
SUBMISSION
SERVANT
My orders would normally go without question... But as I owe thee a debt of gratitude, rather than orders...

...this work shall be given to thee as a threat.
...
Work for you ...?

—would get mad at me like that, I thought ...
Or she'd find it strange—that was the kind of reaction I was expecting, but...
...
Aye, I thought thou might ask...
I understand how thou feelest.
Huh?
You—understand ...?
Once, I was invited to be a god, but I declined.
A GOD ?!
We all feel the same desire... to remain as one is.

Why did you...
...turn me into a vampire?
Can I...
...ever go back to being human?
She—

Fool!!
Dost thou not so much as understand how great an honor thou hast now?!

PAT
ナデ
PAT
ナデ
PAT
ナデ

Aye.
Very well.

It seems as though vampires operate under different rules.
STROKE
さわ
STROKE
さわ

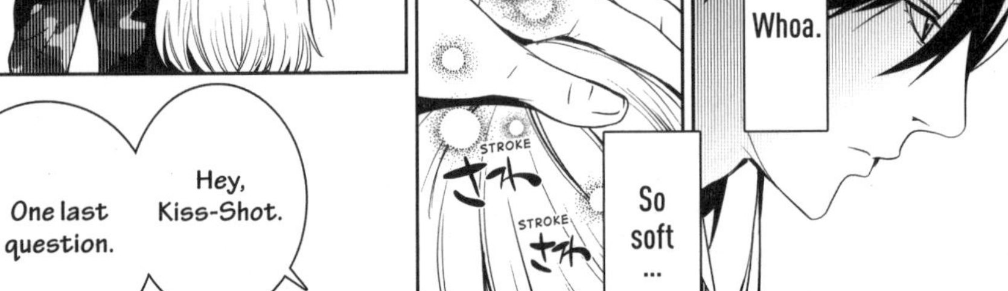
STROKE
さわ
Whoa.
STROKE
さわ
STROKE
さわ
So soft ...
Hey, Kiss-Shot.
One last question.

ZMF
As proof of thy sub-mission to me, stroke my head.
...
Strok-ing your head ...
...proves my sub-mission to you ...?
Dost thou not even know that?!
How ignorant.

That said, don't thou dare get carried away, servant.
... Servant ?!
Even in this state, I am a legendary vampire who has now lived for five hundred years!
A newly born vampire such as thou would have no right to speak to me even if I was not thy master!
Master ?!

... Uh ... Right ...
Somehow, I don't really mind that...
I wonder why that is...?
What is the matter ?
Thou saved my life—rescued me.
And that is why I will grant thee permission to address me in a manner so uncouth and disparaging.
But I will make clear who the superior one is here!

And wait... Kiss-Shot.
Why do you look like that in the first place?
Thy blood alone was not nearly enough.
I was able to at least form these limbs, but they are empty inside...

...
Kiss-Shot?
Did I not tell thee to call me Heart-Under-Blade?
Huh?
That's way too long. I'd trip over the name twice before I was done.

What... so I can't call you that?
Yes... I suppose thou mayest.
... Well...
If that is what pleases thee, then so be it.
I've no reason to refuse.
THP
THP
THP

LUNKHEAD
GLOOMY
DUMMY
DRAMATURGY
GUILLOTINE CUTTER
EPISODE
And... who's that little guy there?
Hm.
Thou art unaware?

This is Batty, mine adorable mascot.
WHAT KIND OF HALF-ASSED MASCOT IS THAT?!
It seemed natural to introduce him here, and I was told it would appeal to the masses.
FWAP
FWAP
TOLD BY WHOM?!
FWAP

But now that I give it more thought, we need not rely on such creatures amidst my presence.
Begone.
BOOM
PYAAAGH
WUH...WAIT, HOLD ON A SECOND! NOW I'M STARTING TO FEEL LIKE WE NEED HIM AROUND!
YOU KNOW, IT'S KINDA... DREARY IN HERE! BRING HIM OUT!
I shan't.
C'MON, BRING HIM OUT! YOU EVEN GAVE HIM A NAME AND EVERYTHING!
Never-more.

Wait... Then... You're...
Indeed I am.

I am none other than the iron-blooded, hot-blooded, yet cold-blooded vampire ...
...Kiss-Shot Acerola-Orion Heart-Under-Blade. Thou mayest call me Heart-Under-Blade.
Pu!

キュ
SKREEK
キュ
SKREEK
キュ
SKREEK
MARKER
Episode.
Guillotine cutter.
And
Dramaturgy.
LUNKHEAD
GLOOMY
DUMMY
DRAMATURGY
GUILLOT
EPISODE
Pu!
They are the ones who took my limbs from me.

Coming right up—after a word from our sponsor.

Under-stood.
YOU'RE TAKING THAT AS AN ANSWER?!

JAKK
"What's the difference between a man and a monkey?"

GRIND
You have five seconds to answer.
FIVE-FOUR-THREE-TWO-ONE —
Your answer?
SKRAKK
GRIND

ZZZT
Could you wait a moment, Episode?
I also have a question for the young lady there.
Of course, it's the same thing I ask everyone I meet for the first time.

Hey.
Since when were you and I ever friendly enough to let you do *this*?

"Fucking slut."

So I thought... I must have said something to upset you.
...I see. Well, that's mighty impressive.
I guess that puts me at ease.
You're just special, that's all.
GCCHT
GCCHT
GCCHT
GCCHT
GRRRK

KCCHT

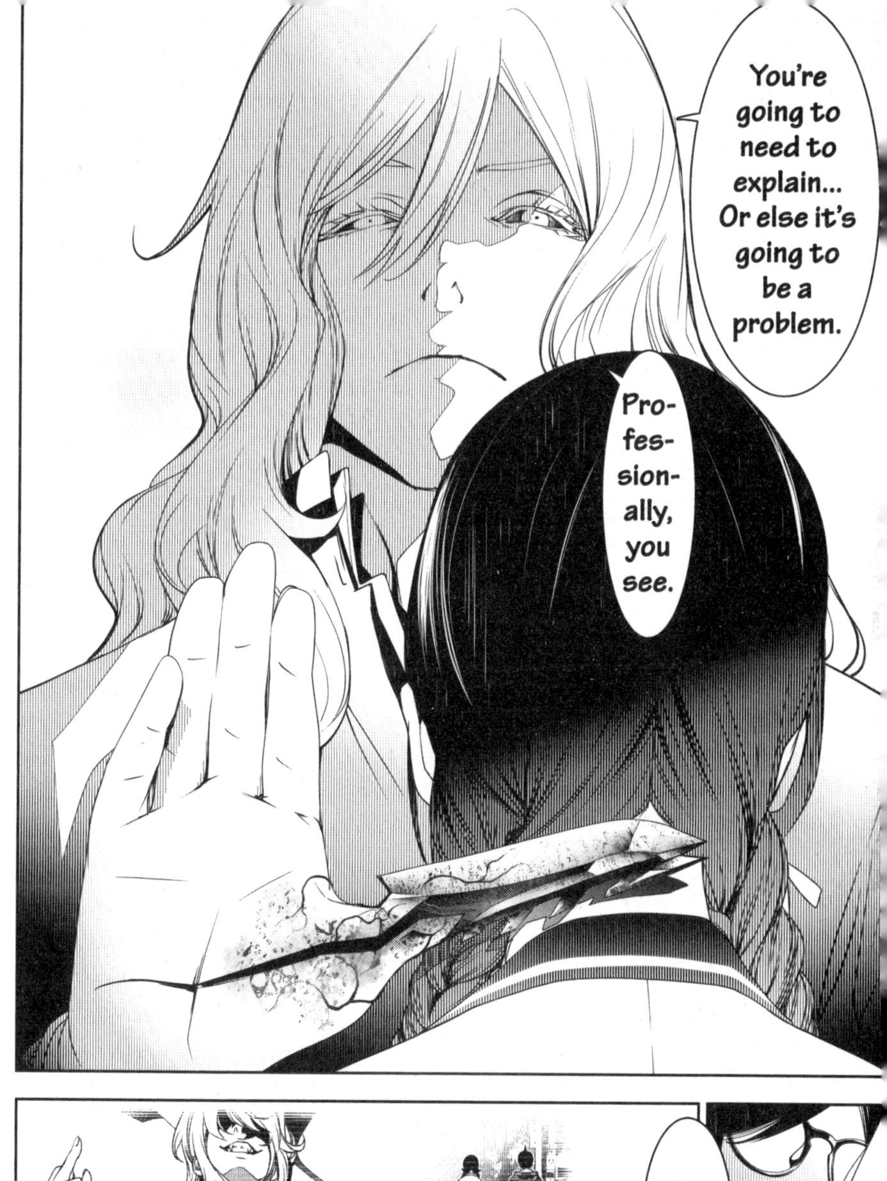

You're going to need to explain... Or else it's going to be a problem.
Pro-fes-sion-ally, you see.

The other day...
We happened to cross paths, right?
—It was then.
I won-dered what it was you said.

So you know about that.
How'd you figure I'm from *that* particular country?
What was it?
Is there a map with a big X on it stuck to my face or something?
Everyone east of India looks the exact same to me.
So how the hell were you able to pinpoint a country as minor as that one?

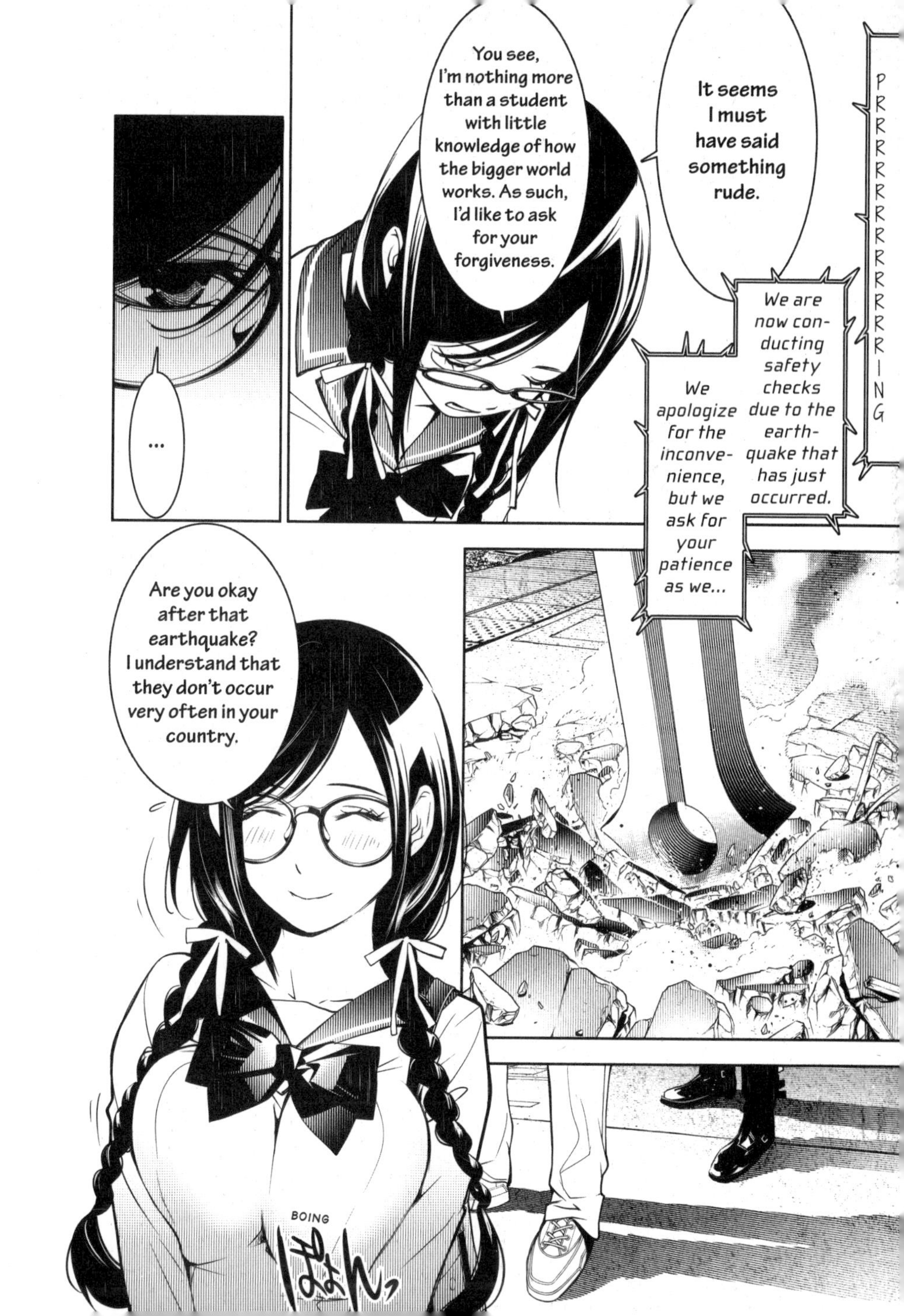
PRRRRRRRRRRRRING
It seems I must have said something rude.
You see, I'm nothing more than a student with little knowledge of how the bigger world works. As such, I'd like to ask for your forgiveness.
...
We are now conducting safety checks due to the earthquake that has just occurred.
We apologize for the inconvenience, but we ask for your patience as we...
Are you okay after that earthquake? I understand that they don't occur very often in your country.
BOING
ぽよんっ

205RNM2
—PK
205RN02
—PK
I'm very sorry.
めうえなかまち
Meue-nakamachi

BAKEMONOGATARI 9

BAKEMONOGATARI 9

Hold up there.
BZZT
Little Miss Melons.
BZZT

BLOOP

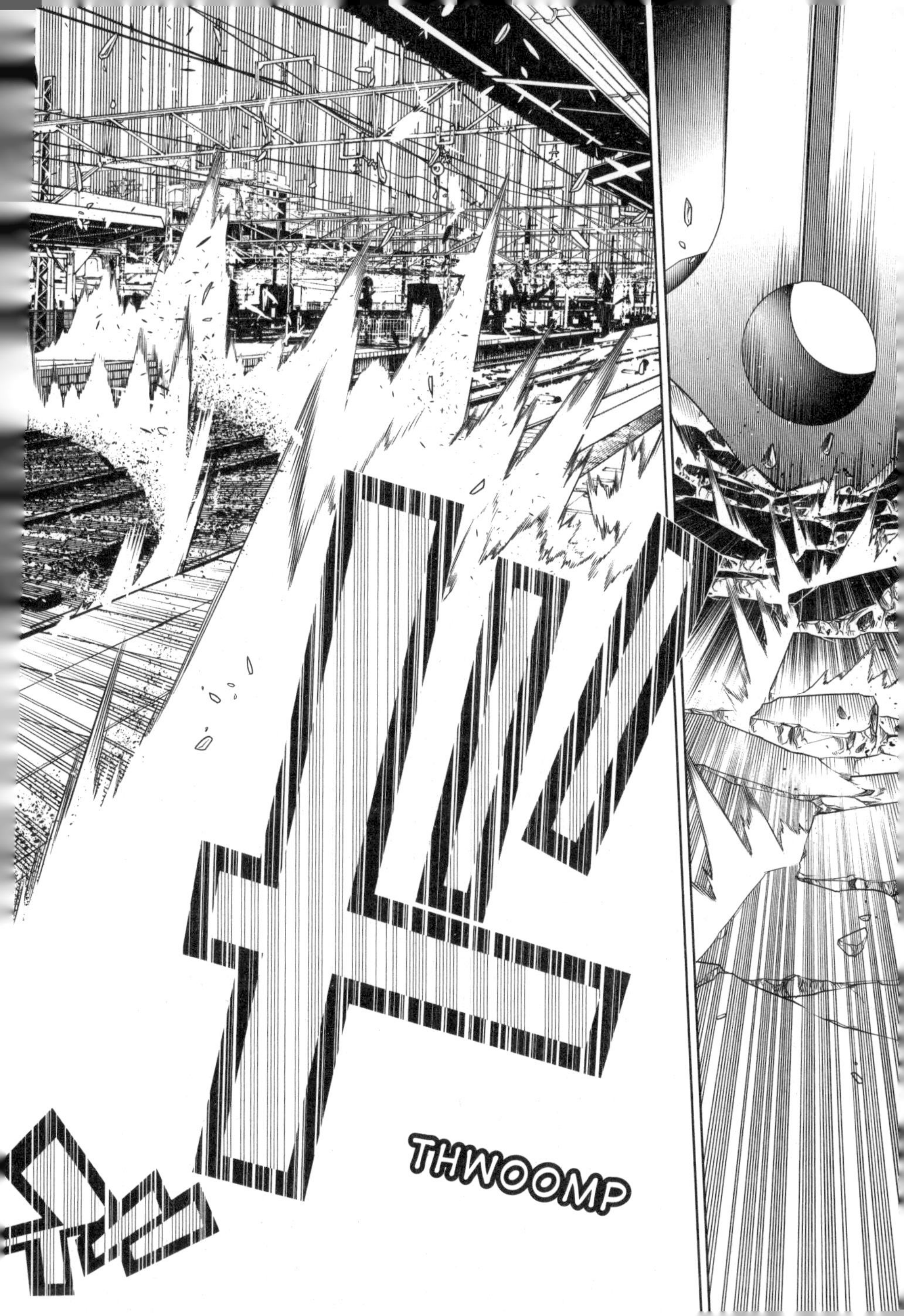
THWOOMP

A greeting. Very important.
How upstanding of you.
But I wouldn't call you an upstanding person.
Not to our eyes.
TH-THNK
TH-THNK
TH-THNK
TH-THNK
Gotta love it.

I'll admit I didn't expect to get my hands on spoils like these.
I mean, we plucked off all four of Heart-Under-Blade's limbs.
PSSSSHT
I got the left arm, Mister Dramaturgy got her right arm, and you got her legs...
Still a pretty big payday even if we left this place now. Right, Guillotine Cutter?
Hello.
Not that I even want to know what you'll be using those legs for—

Still... The signal I'm getting is very weak.
It'll be hard to capture her like this.
She's on the brink of death... But in this case,
there may be something in the way—like a barrier of some sort. Perhaps she's in a special building.
BMMF
That so?
Whatever. I'm fine with calling it here myself.
PRRRRRRING
You may never get another chance like this in your entire life, even if you live for centuries,
Episode.
THMP
Hah.
BAM
1

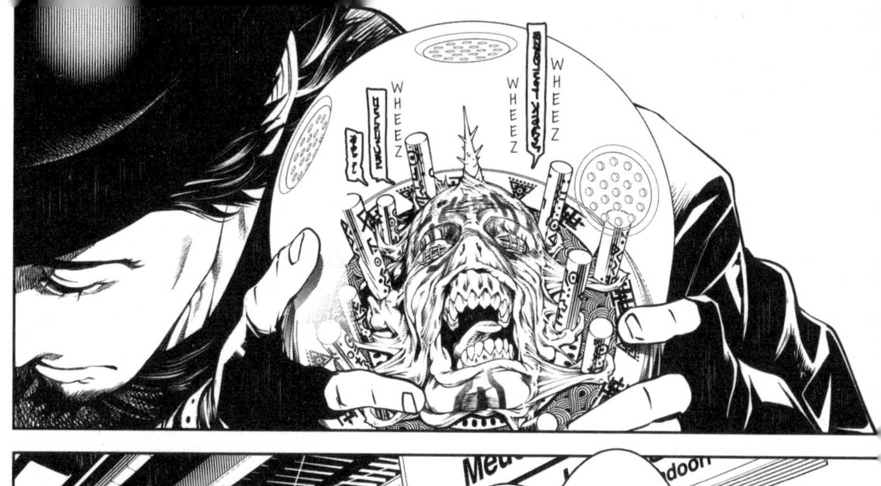
WHEEZ
WHEEZ
WHEEZ

...Seems this was all for naught.
It did look like she'd leaped all the way to this area.
Hah.
To Oyama
To Urabe
So that grubby old hag is still there? Guess she never left that town.
Gotta love it.

Welcome to the world of the night.
She laughed.
It was a spine-chilling cackle.

... ...!

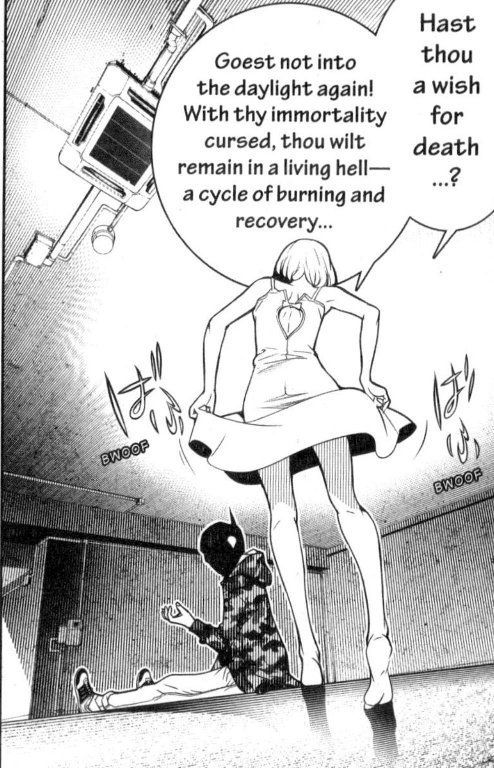

Hast thou a wish for death ...?
Goest not into the daylight again! With thy immortality cursed, thou wilt remain in a living hell—a cycle of burning and recovery...
BWOOF
BWOOF

I... I'm ... ...!
A vampire now...?

The look in her eyes seemed to chide me for stating the obvious.

And then— she laughed.

My thrall.

YOU FOOL !!!
FZZT
FZZT
FZZT

What manner of dunce runneth out under the sun without warning?!
'Twas but a moment that I took mine eyes off of thee ...!
Agh... How weight-ful!
ZZT
ZZZT

KRAK
KRAK
KRAK
SIZZLE
SIZZLE
SIZZLE

SST

AAAAAHHHH
ゴロ
ROLL
ゴロ
ROLL
ゴロ
ROLL
ゴロ
ROLL

...!
ZWOOF
SIZ-ZLE
BFZZZZZT
SIZ-ZLE
SIZ-ZLE
SIZ-ZLE

ZWOOF
KRAKL
KRAK
KRAK
?!!
...?

HYAA-AAA-AAA-AGH
PYA-AA-AGH
Tch!

BWOOF

Huh?

I have Hanekawa's contact information on my phone.
In other words, those panties weren't just a dream.
Oh... So this is a school.
A cram school, I guess.

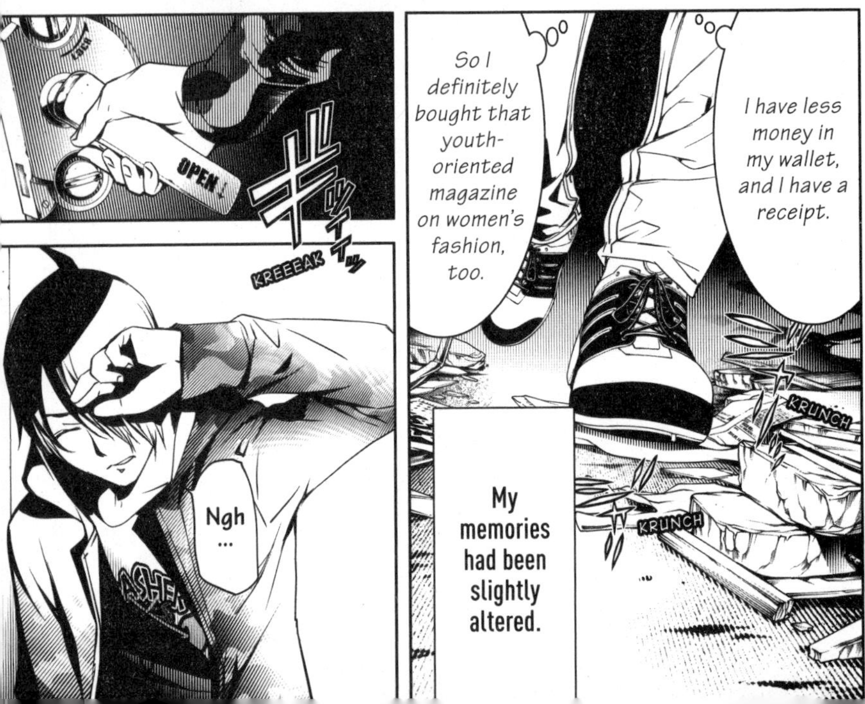
I have less money in my wallet, and I have a receipt.
So I definitely bought that youth-oriented magazine on women's fashion, too.
KRUNCH
KRUNCH
My memories had been slightly altered.
OPEN
KREEEAK
Ngh ...

She's about... ten years old? Blonde... Pale skin. ...Maybe she's not Japanese?
I'm innocent ... I have to be, right...?
Wait, putting that aside for now,
the phrase "alone in an abandoned building with a young girl I don't know" has an impossibly criminal scent to it...
TAP TAP TAP TAP
It's ... 4:32 PM.
So bright ...!
Hm?
Did I set my phone's backlight to be this bright?
16:32
March 28
Oh. Still after-noon...
However hands-off my parents might be, two nights without any contact is pushing it.
Where's the exit... Up here?
Huh ?!
Crap !!
KLAT
M...March 28?! Two days have passed already...?!

H...HEY... WUH-WAKE UP! WHO ARE YOU?!
POKE
...
Nnh.
...Five more minutes ...
FWOOF
GNNNNH!!
MY NOS-TRILS!
...WAIT, NO! I SAID, GET UP ALREADY!!

...Just "x" more minutes.
HOW MUCH LONGER IS THAT?!
4.6 billion years or so?
THAT'D BE ENOUGH TIME TO CREATE ANOTHER EARTH!

あは
HUU
ああ
UUU
ああ
?あ
あ
UNH?!

OH!! IT WAS ALL A DREAM !!
I tried yelling that out.

Of course, it wasn't a dream—because if it had been,
I would have awoken in the comfort of my own room.

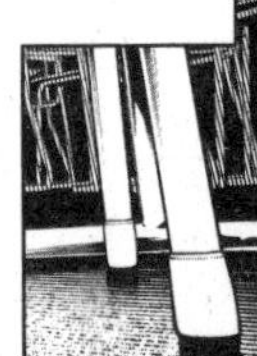

What is this place? ...An abandoned building?
...

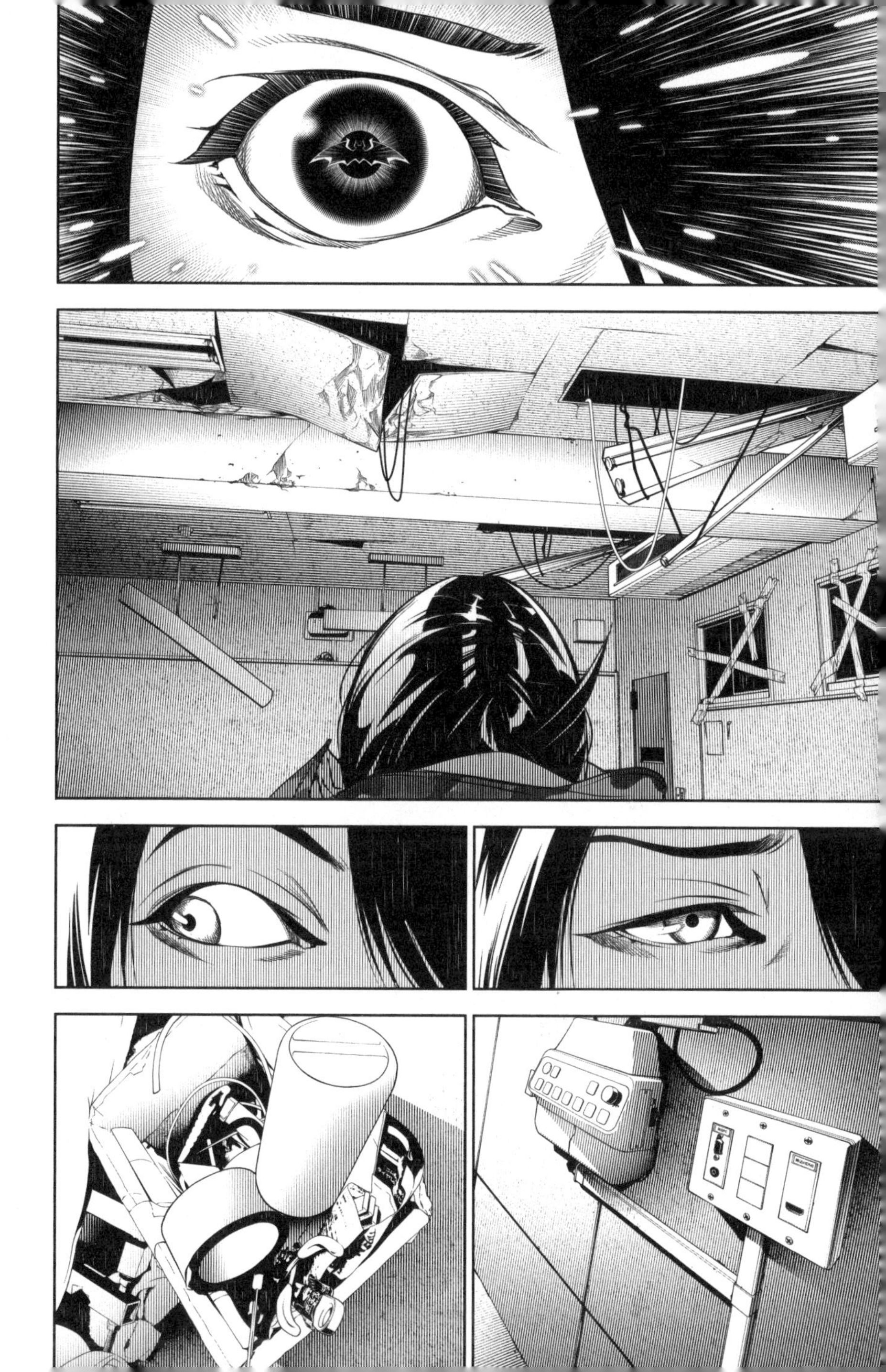

I was sure ...

...that this would result in my death.
A happy ending to my life.
It *seemed* like the logical outcome of giving away all the blood in your body.

But—
I wasn't expect-ing *this* ...
I was hardly prepared ...
...for what came next.

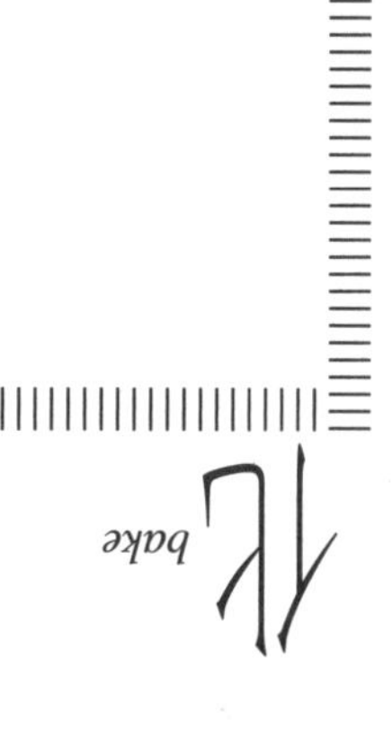

物 mono

KOYOMIvamp

9

語 gatari

物 *mono*

KOYOMIvamp

9

語 *gatari*

I remembered the only friend I had in this world.

Thank you...
I'm speculating here, but this may have been the first time in her life that...
...Kiss-Shot Acerola-Orion Heart-Under-Blade gave someone her thanks.
I instantly began to lose conscious-ness.
And then, with my last wisp of awareness, I—

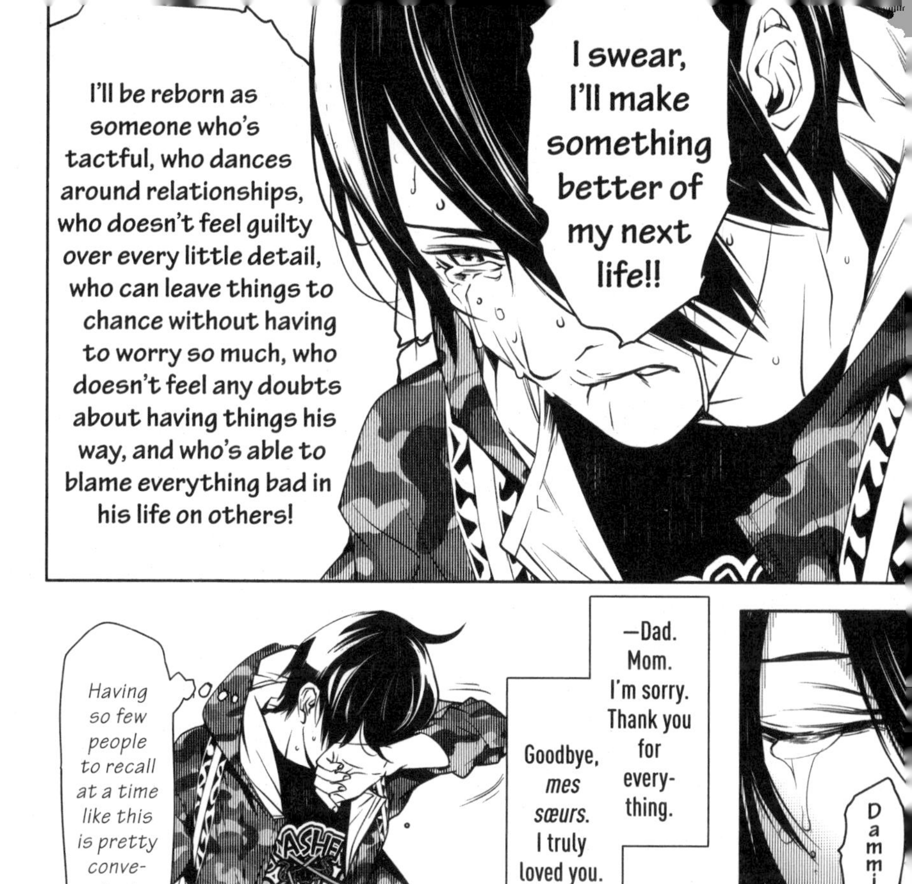
I swear, I'll make something better of my next life!!
I'll be reborn as someone who's tactful, who dances around relationships, who doesn't feel guilty over every little detail, who can leave things to chance without having to worry so much, who doesn't feel any doubts about having things his way, and who's able to blame everything bad in his life on others!
Dammit…
—Dad. Mom. I'm sorry. Thank you for every-thing.
Goodbye, *mes sœurs*. I truly loved you.
Having so few people to recall at a time like this is pretty conve-nient.

Th-

...then I should die so this beautiful creature may live.
Go ahead. Suck.
I'll save you. Suck my blood.
I'll give it all to you. Don't leave a single drop—wring me dry.
...
Ah.
...Really...?

Unh ... Ah—
Sorry...
...
I'm sorry...
TWITCH
TWITCH
SKREE
Don't give up, stupid!!
Dammit!
How did things end up this way—? Well...of course I know how.
Dammit.
Dammit!
What reason did I have to bother staying alive? I didn't really have one.
There was no beauty in it—nothing pretty about it. And if that was my life...

Haah!
Haah!
Haah!
Hfff!
Eventu-
ally...
Oww
...!
...I stopped
hearing
her voice.
Only
the
pain
was
left.
Almost
as if it
blamed
me.

AAAAAAAAAHHHH
I forced my frozen legs to move—and traveled pretty far.
As if to cast something off. As if to forget it all.
GSSHNK
GSSHNK
GSSHNK
GSSHNK
GSSHNK
GSSHNK
She made so much noise back there. Her screams were so loud.
GKKT
OOSATO INN
Daagh!
It doesn't have to be me. Someone else... Someone else can take my place—

I don't think ...I'm allowed to let this beautiful vampire die in such an ungraceful way.
I—I...

I've never even donated blood before, and now I'm going to let her drink all the blood in my body?

In other words, saving her would be my death.

No... Even then... How am I supposed to save her? She only wants me as an emergency food ration...!!

Ngh !!!
—Stop it.

I'll do any-thing if you save me!
Really!
I can't stand this!
I'm sorry! I'm sorry!
WRIGGLE
WRIGGLE
WRIGGLE

That's... not *who you are*—right? It can't be.
You're not someone who'd... plead and apologize to someone like me—
You shouldn't be permitted to do something like that.

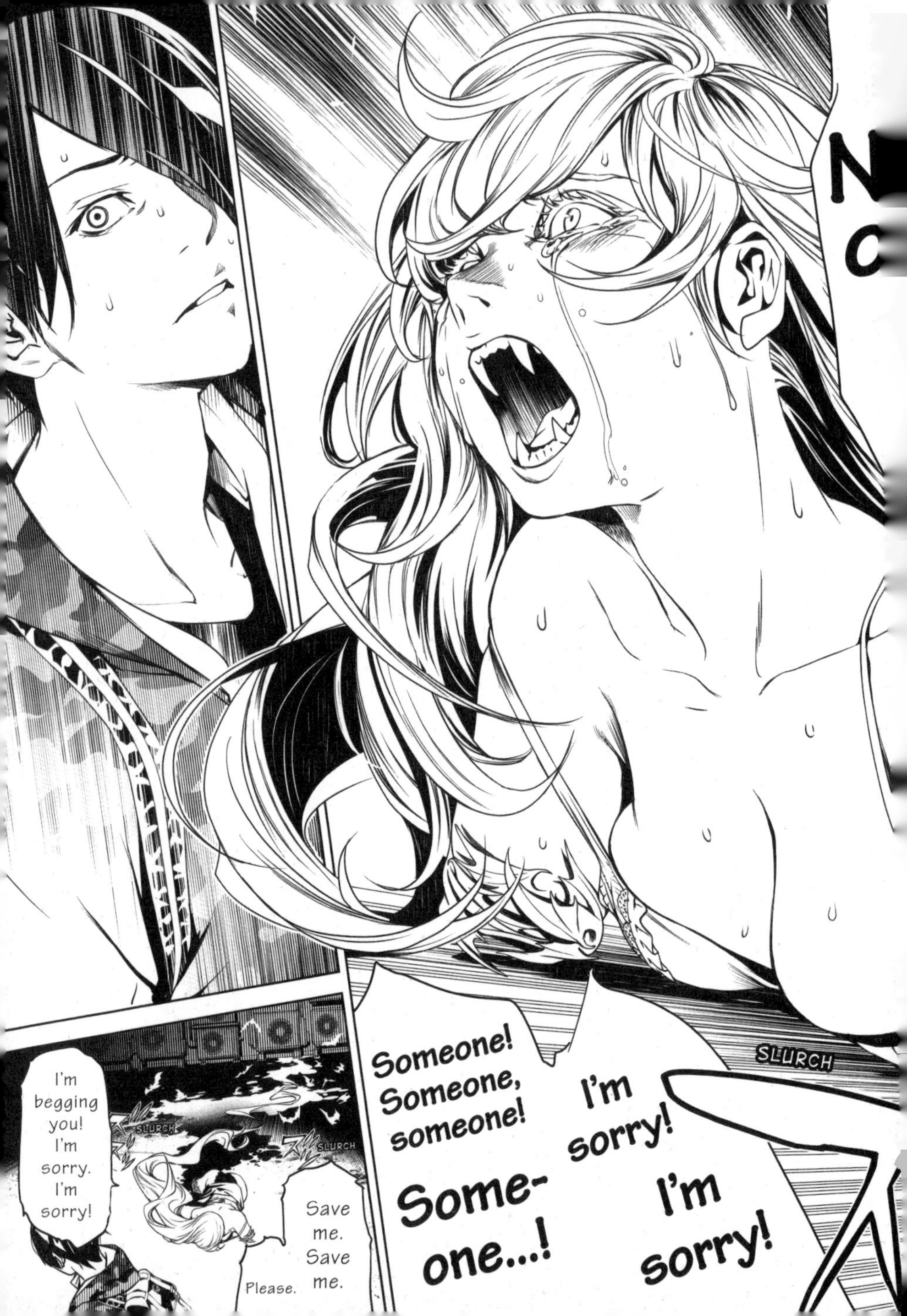

NO
SLURCH
Someone! Someone, someone!
I'm sorry!
Some-one...!
I'm sorry!
SLURCH
SLURCH
Save me. Save me.
Please.
I'm begging you! I'm sorry. I'm sorry!

No! No! I don't wanna die!
SLURCH
Save me! Save me!
I don't want to die!
I don't want to die!
SLURCH
no, no, no !!
SLURCH

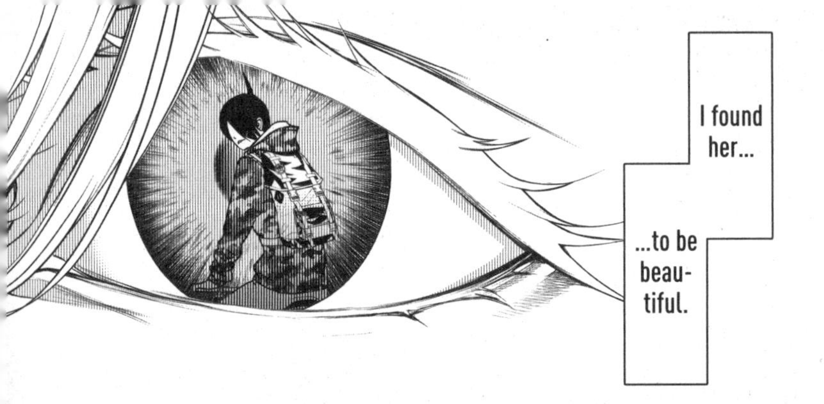
I found her...
...to be beau-tiful.

I was instantly under her spell.

I couldn't take my eyes off her.
I was frozen in my tracks—unable to move my legs from that spot.
I don't want to die
Save me
Please
I'm sorry
No
Someone
I don't want to die
CRASHER

Unh—
BLUP

...
SHIVER
That voice ...
Dost thou mean to say...
...thou wilt not... aid me...?

SLURCH
She suddenly sounds so frail... All the coldness and harshness...
All the irreverence and arrogance of someone who only sees me as food has vanished...

SCREEK
Su—
...Surely, thou jest...?

Nay... What would be the meaning in pulverizing him here...?
Not this... No...
Unh—
Unngh!
KRAK
KRAK
KRAK

Nay... I lack... blood...
My judg-ment... is...!
GRAKK
THONK
THONK
Eegh!
GKKT
GKKT
GKKT

GZZT
GZZT
GZZT
GZZT
GZZT
GZZZZT
Ah—
KRAKL

GRA-
KRAKK

You may be thinking, "You're dragging this Hanekawa's panties thing out way too long."
...And I wouldn't fault you for that.
But you see, if I hadn't recalled Hanekawa's panties...
...then my life surely would have ended here.
One might say I'm deeply indebted to Hanekawa ('s panties) for that.
SHIIINE

Saka
ひがしまちにし
Higashimachi-nishi
Urabe
To Oyama
Meue-nakamachi
Chapter 0
Koyomi Vamp
BOOK DESIGN
VEIA

THE STORY SO FAR
It shall be...
...thy privilege to aid me.
Together with Suruga Kanbaru, Koyomi Araragi is able to successfully save Nadeko Sengoku from a "snake" aberration, though not without a struggle. It is now June 13, and life is peaceful once more, causing Koyomi to recall the events of the spring break that began it all. That spring break was a time of firsts—his first meeting with Tsubasa Hanekawa, his first encounter with the wound-covered vampire Kiss-Shot Acerola-Orion Heart-Under-Blade, and the beginning of the living hell that only just ended for Koyomi...

MAIN CHARACTERS
Koyomi Araragi
A boy who one day encountered a beautiful yet wound-covered vampire. The protagonist of this story, who now looks back to tell its tale of wounds.
Tsubasa Hanekawa
Koyomi's classmate and an honor student that no honor could sufficiently describe. When she happens to meet Koyomi, she begins to feel concerned and goes out of her way to talk to him in hopes of becoming his friend.
Kiss-Shot Acerola-Orion Heart-Under-Blade
A noble, haughty, beautiful, iron-blooded, hot-blooded, yet cold-blooded vampire. She seeks help from Koyomi when he happens to pass her by on the ground, covered in wounds and with her limbs torn off.

BAKEMONOGATARI

OH!GREAT
ORIGINAL STORY:
NISIOISIN
ORIGINAL CHARACTER
DESIGN: VOFAN

9